THE STORY OF
DISNEY

JOHN PASSARO

SMART APPLE MEDIA MANKATO MINNESOTA

Published by Smart Apple Media

123 South Broad Street, Mankato, Minnesota 56001

Copyright © 2000 Smart Apple Media.
International copyrights reserved in all countries.
No part of this book may be reproduced in any form without written
permission from the publisher.

Produced by The Creative Spark, San Juan Capistrano, CA
  Editor: Elizabeth Sirimarco
  Designer: Mary Francis-DeMarois
  Art Direction: Robert Court
  Page Layout: Jo Maurine Wheeler

Photo credits: Corbis/Jonathan Blair 4, 34; Reuters/HO/Archive Photos 6;
Delip Mehta/Contact Press Images/PNI 7; Corbis/Bettmann 8, 19, 22, 29;
Reuters/Sam Mircovich/Archive Photos 9; Corbis/Robbie Jack 10; Gene
Lester/Archive Photos 12; Corbis/Vince Streano 13; Archive Photos/PNI 14,
21; Corbis/Morton Beebe, S.F. 16; Archive Photos 17; Corbis/Hulton-Deutsch
Collection 18; Gary Matoso/Contact Press Images/PNI 23; Jan Neubauer/
Rainbow/PNI 24; Corbis/Kevin Fleming 26; Andre Jenny/Stock South/PNI 27;
Ben Van Hook/Black Star/PNI 30, 32; Corbis/Michael S. Yamashita 31; Corbis
/Michael Gerber 33; Corbis/Natalie Fobes 36; Corbis/Neal Preston 37; Jerome
Friar/Impact Visuals/PNI 38; Reuters/Jeff Christensen/Archive 39; Willie
Hill/Stock, Boston/PNI 40

Library of Congress Cataloging-in-Publication Data

Passaro, John, 1953–
     The story of The Walt Disney Company / by John Passaro.
     p. cm. — (Spirit of success)
   Includes index.
   SUMMARY: Traces the story of the world-famous Walt Disney Company from
its founding to the present and discusses the man responsible for creating it.
   ISBN 1-58340-002-8 (alk. paper)
   1. Walt Disney Company—History—Juvenile literature. [1. Walt Disney
Company—History. 2. Disney, Walt, 1901-1966.] I. Title. II. Series.
   PN1999.W27 P37 1999
   384'.8'06579494—dc21

                                                                         98-48719

9   8   7   6   5   4   3   2

Table of Contents

Disney Today

I n July 1923, Walt Disney left home to join his older
brother Roy in Hollywood, California. He brought with
him nothing more than a few cartoon drawings, a
used suit, and $40. Roy had saved up about $250. Together
they borrowed $500 more to set up a studio. The Disney
brothers were going to make cartoons, also called
animated films. They bought a second-hand camera to
create them. Next, they rented a small space and put a
sign in the window that read "Disney Brothers Studio."

Few people knew about the small business, but the Disney brothers had plenty of creativity—and a lot of determination.

Disney Brothers Studio eventually became the Walt Disney Company, a world-famous corporation. It grew from making a few hundred dollars in 1923 to more than $23 billion in 1998. Even today, many people first think of the popular animated films produced by the company when they hear the Disney® name. While the film studio is still at the heart of the Walt Disney Company, it is involved in many more entertainment projects as well.

Many visitors travel to Disneyland® in California or Disney World® in Florida, but these popular tourist destinations are only one part of the Walt Disney Company. It also runs amusement parks in both Japan and France. Florida's EPCOT Center® (EPCOT stands for Experimental Prototype Community of Tomorrow) allows visitors to venture into the future and travel to foreign lands. Just down the road is Disney's Animal Kingdom™, which opened in 1998. Visitors to Disney's Animal Kingdom can view more than 1,000 animals from around the world, as well as exhibits about dinosaurs and other extinct creatures. Visitors to the various Disney theme parks spent more than five billion dollars in 1997 alone.

That same year, Disney received almost $11 billion in **royalties.** People and companies who use pictures of Disney characters, show Disney movies, play Disney music, or otherwise use Disney's property must pay a fee to the

animated films

Drawings produced on film and then shown through a projector. Animated films are also called cartoons.

royalties

Money paid to a company (or person) in exchange for using its property.

Roy E. Disney, nephew of Walt Disney, takes a tour around Animal Kingdom, the latest Disney theme park.

Walt Disney Company. Millions of boys and girls—as well as adults—in most corners of the world know and love Mickey Mouse®, Donald Duck®, Goofy®, and the many other famous Disney characters. This means many companies want to feature their pictures on a product.

When Americans watch television, many of them tune into a Disney production. Disney owns the ABC® television **network,** with stations across the United States. Disney also owns hundreds of cable companies. Besides the Disney Channel®, the Walt Disney Company also enjoys part ownership in cable networks such as the History Channel®, Arts and Entertainment® (A&E), Lifetime Television®, and E! Entertainment Television®.

network

A television or cable company that produces programs to be shown on local stations across a large territory. The ABC network, for example, broadcasts its programs on stations all over the United States.

A young fan wears Disney's famous mouse ears and a pair of Mickey Mouse sunglasses. If a company wants to use a picture of Mickey Mouse on its products, it first must ask permission from the Walt Disney Company.

From Idea to Screen

The word animation means to create life. Artists draw many thousands of individual pictures. Next, they connect the pictures together. When they run the series of pictures through a projector at high speed, the drawings appear to move. The pictures aren't really moving, of course. The human eye fills in the gaps so that a lion, for example, appears to be running through the jungle.

Young artists can create their own animation by drawing a stick-figure lion in the corner of a pad of paper. On the next pages of the pad, legs are drawn in a position slightly forward from the position on the pages before. When quickly fanning the pages of the pad, the lion appears to be walking!

Disney has also started television stations and cable channels in many other parts of the world as well. Companies that advertised their products on Disney television and cable stations paid the Walt Disney

The Walt Disney Company named its hockey team The Mighty Ducks in honor of one of its most popular movies.

Actors portray the two main characters in Disney's stage production of Beauty and the Beast.

Company more than $6 billion in 1997.

For sports fans, there's the Mighty Ducks® of Anaheim, the National Hockey League® team owned by Disney. Hundreds of other sports can be seen on ESPN® and ESPN 2®, two more Disney networks. *Monday Night Football*®, an ABC program, belongs to Disney as well. Lifetime Television network runs women's ice hockey and basketball games.

During a single week near the end of 1997, more than 34 million people watched *The Wonderful World of Disney*® on television; 3.3 million kids watched Saturday-morning Disney television; 3.6 million people watched the Disney Channel; and almost 3 million people listened to Disney Radio®. Almost 800,000 visitors bought tickets to Disney theme parks, and another 800,000 people bought products at the Disney stores. Disney sent 9 million copies of the Christmas version of *Beauty and the Beast* to video stores. Theatergoers by the thousands saw the stage production of *Beauty and the Beast* on Broadway in New York City. *Beauty and the Beast* played in England, Germany, Mexico, and Japan as well. To put it simply, Disney is nearly everywhere in the entertainment world.

The Walt Disney Company is one of many businesses that developed from the vision and work of only a few people. In this case, the person most responsible for Disney's success was Walter Elias Disney. It is impossible to tell the story of the Walt Disney Company without telling his story as well.

Making a Cartoon

   Animation artists begin with an idea for a story, and then they write a script of what will happen. Once the writers have worked out a plot for their story, sound artists plan a musical script. Usually specialists create all the sound — including voices, sound effects, and background music — before the animation work begins. This way, artists can carefully match the action to sound.

   The artists sketch their ideas on story boards where they draw the action for each scene. They make their first drawings, called conceptual drawings, of what the film and its characters will look like. Artists work on the characters for many hours to create different emotions and movements. Usually artists mold three-dimensional models out of clay so that the animators can see how the character would look from any angle. Then layout artists design the settings, the action, and the camera angles and shots.

Finally, a group of animators draws the backgrounds, characters, and special effects in pencil. Sometimes one animator supervises many artists working on just one character. When everyone finishes their work, they run the pencil drawings through a test to check if the animation works as planned. If everything looks good, clean-up artists finish the animation. They make the final color pictures based on the pencil drawings. When the artists finally combine the animation with sound, the film is ready for the movie theaters.

Today's animation films are usually created with the help of computers, but some things will never change. Creativity and imagination are still the keys to any successful film.

Mickey Mouse and Walt Disney

A multibillion-dollar company seldom starts at the top, and success doesn't always come quickly. Sometimes a company's founders struggle for many years before achieving their goals. Walt Elias Disney had his share of hard times before he found success.

Walt's family wasn't stable when he was growing up, and it wasn't always loving. The Disneys often moved from one place to another. When Walter was born in 1901, his family lived in Chicago, Illinois. Then they moved to a farm in Marceline, Missouri. Within several months, the family sold the farm and moved into town. Three years later, they moved to Kansas City.

Life was often difficult at the Disney home because Walt's father, Elias, was a troubled, angry man. He often beat Walt, his three brothers, and their sister. Despite all Walt's future success, many people believe these harsh beginnings haunted him throughout his life.

Walt's career didn't begin smoothly. His first job as a commercial artist for $50 a month ended quickly. Next, at age 19, he started his first company with a friend named Ubbe Iwerks, who would be Walt's lifelong partner. Iwerks-Disney Commercial Artists, as they called the company, lasted only one month before they accepted offers to work for the Kansas City Slide Company. When they saved enough money to go out on their own again, Walt and Ubbe started another company, which they called Laugh-O-Gram Films. Within a year, Laugh-O-Gram Films was officially forced into **bankruptcy** because Walt and Ubbe didn't make enough money to pay their bills.

Some people believe that Walt could be difficult to work with. He expected others to work as hard as he did. Sometimes he had a difficult time letting coworkers do their jobs without interfering. Early in his career, he became seriously ill and was hospitalized. Doctors told him it was because he worked too hard.

bankruptcy

When a company (or individual) cannot pay its debts, it may be forced to go out of business. It then pays creditors with any money that is left. This process is called bankruptcy.

Today the Disney company produces films at its studios in Burbank. Walt Disney had a difficult time at the beginning of his career, but the company he started earned $23 billion in 1998.

Walt Disney considered his difficulties and decided to keep a positive attitude. He simply wouldn't accept failure. From the beginning, he was dedicated to creativity. One legend says he drew and sketched from the time he was seven years old. Some say he drew on toilet paper using coal because his family couldn't afford nice drawing paper and pencils. He may have sold his first drawing at age seven to neighbors. As a teenager during World War I, Walt served as an ambulance driver in the Red Cross. He camouflaged his ambulance with cartoons from bumper to bumper.

In 1923, Walt decided to move to Hollywood and make films with his brother Roy. The two signed a contract with a company in New York to make cartoons. They worked in a room in the back of a real-estate office. Walt created the animation drawings, his brother worked the camera, and they hired two young women to paint the **celluloid,** the clear film the projector light shines through to project images onto a movie screen.

celluloid

A clear, plastic film that resists high temperatures. The celluloid sheets are painted then photographed on film.

Walt Disney pauses for a moment while sketching Mickey Mouse. Mickey first appeared in movies in 1928 when Disney Studios introduced Steamboat Willie.

In 1924, Ubbe Iwerks moved to California to take over the animation duties. For five years, the Disney brothers and Ubbe Iwerks struggled to get enough work just to pay themselves and their few employees. From time to time, it looked like they wouldn't make it.

Walt wouldn't quit. Throughout all his early difficulties, he knew that his life's work would be animation and entertainment. After five long years of fighting to survive, the Walt Disney Studio got a big break. Walt was returning by train to California from New York City. He had tried to find work for the company in the city but had little luck.

Walt Disney and a camera operator film a penguin. By closely studying an animal, Walt believed an animator could draw more realistic pictures. In 1930, he hoped to capture the movement and behavior of penguins for the Disney cartoon, Peculiar Penguins.

Young actress Shirley Temple attends a Disney premiere with two of the characters from Snow White and the Seven Dwarfs.

He was sketching in his drawing book, looking for new ideas, when suddenly he had an inspiration: Walt created a cartoon character named Mickey Mouse®.

When Walt created and developed Mickey Mouse, he saved the Disney Brothers Studio. As Walt himself said, "Mickey Mouse popped out of my mind and onto a drawing pad on a train ride at a time when the business fortunes of my brother Roy and myself were low and disaster seemed right around the corner...the little fellow provided the means for expanding our organization."

Walt and Roy had the good business sense and the creative talent to turn Mickey into the foundation of everything that was to come. Even Mickey Mouse, however, had a rough start in life.

The film industry was just beginning in the United States. At the time, movies were black and white with no sound. Mickey Mouse was supposed to make his first appearance in a silent film called *Plane Crazy,* but in the meantime, sound came to the movies. Disney regrouped, set aside *Plane Crazy,* and made a short film called *Steamboat Willie* instead.

Steamboat Willie debuted in 1928. It was the world's first sound cartoon. Walt himself supplied Mickey's squeaky voice. Disney's New York distributor made sure the film was in theaters nationwide. Almost overnight, millions of Mickey Mouse fans were born. In 1930, Mickey had his first comic-strip adventure in *Lost on a Desert Island.* Walt wrote the strip, and Ubbe drew the pictures. Soon, hundreds of "Mickey Mouse Clubs" sprung up all across the United States. On Saturday afternoons, young people around the country attended club meetings held at local theaters. They sang Mickey Mouse songs, exchanged souvenirs, and watched the latest cartoons together.

From that point forward, Disney Studios grew on the success of Mickey Mouse. It created many other imaginative cartoon characters, such as Pluto®, Donald Duck®, and Goofy®. It made dozens of creative movies, including

The Mickey Mouse Club *television show debuted in 1955. For 4 years, the program aired every weekday after school. Annette Funicello was one of the most popular "Mouseketeers," as the show's young stars were called. At the peak of the show's popularity, fans bought about 20,000 Mouseketeer caps, which featured Mickey's famous ears, each day.*

Snow White and the Seven Dwarfs, Pinocchio, and *Fantasia.* It produced one of the first color television shows, *The Wonderful World of Color®.*

In 1955, Disneyland® opened in Anaheim, California. It was Walt's attempt to create a place for families to have fun together. Within 10 years, 30 million people had visited Disneyland. By then, Walt was deeply involved in creating two parks in Florida, Disney World® and the EPCOT®, which he imagined as the city of tomorrow, a model of a better place to live and work.

During his lifetime, Walt Disney won 32 Academy Awards, the award given to people in the film industry by the Academy of Motion Picture Arts and Sciences.

Mickey Mouse

Mickey Mouse is an international movie star, but not everyone knows him by the same name. Italians, for example, call him *Topolino,* which means "Little Mouse." Spanish fans call him *El Ratón Mickey*—the Spanish words for Mickey the mouse. Here are a few names for the world's most famous mouse, followed by the language from which they come.

Miki Maus	Bulgarian
Mi Lao Shu	Chinese
Mikki Maous	Greek
Miki Egèr	Hungarian
Miki Tikus	Indonesian
Myszka Mickey	Polish
Musse Pigg	Swedish

Life after Walt

Walt didn't live to see Disney World® or EPCOT® completed. He died of lung cancer in 1966 at the age of 65. His brother Roy became the **chief executive officer (CEO)** of the Walt Disney Company until his death in 1971. Even without the Disney brothers, the company continued to travel along the road Walt and Roy had paved. The company's president from 1971 through 1980, Carl Walker, continued Walt's work on the new theme parks. Disney World opened in October 1971, followed by EPCOT in October 1982.

After Walt Disney died, however, the company had difficulty replacing his creative talent and ideas. The theme parks were successful, but few people at Disney® seemed to have many good ideas for movies. The public began to think of Disney as old-fashioned. Its movies seemed too unrealistic, even a little bit too sweet. The artists, directors, writers, and actors who made films and animated features were no longer interested in Disney movies. The most creative people in Hollywood no longer wanted to work for Disney.

In an effort to get the company moving again, its leaders made a big decision. In 1983, the Walt Disney Company formed Touchstone Pictures®. Instead of making movies that appealed only to children and young families, Touchstone would make movies for young adults and older audiences. The company's films have starred popular actors, such as Tom Cruise, Madonna, Bette Midler, Robert Redford, and Julia Roberts. Some films produced by Touchstone Pictures include *Sister Act,* starring Whoopi Goldberg, *The Preacher's Wife,* starring Whitney Houston, *Armageddon,* starring Ben Affleck and Bruce Willis, and *A Civil Action,* starring John Travolta. The production company even continued Disney's animation work when it made *Who Framed Roger Rabbit.*

chief executive officer (CEO)

The person responsible for managing a company and making decisions that help the company make a profit.

merger

A merger takes place when two companies agree to join forces and become one company.

media

All the different ways of communicating information to the public, including newspapers, television, radio, books, magazines, and movies.

publicly traded company

A company that sells shares of stock to the public in order to earn money for its business.

stock

Shared ownership in a company by many people who buy shares, or portions, of stock, hoping that the company will make a profit.

became the largest entertainment company in the world when it bought Capital Cities/ABC television network for about $19 billion in a **merger.** After the merger, Disney owned all the ABC television programs, Capital Records, and many other entertainment **media.**

Disney's business now included owning and managing other people's creative property, as well as making movies. Once again, talented musicians, artists, actors, and directors began flocking to Disney to make music, cartoons, and films.

Disney has become so large that it is organized into many companies. Each has its own job to do and its own president. One Disney company works only on feature-length animated films, while another creates live-action movies. Another company manages Disneyland® and the other theme parks. Separate Disney companies produce plays for the theater, manage the television stations, and handle the cable companies. Disney's music company works on producing popular music. Its publishing company creates books that feature popular Disney characters.

Where did Disney get the money to buy other companies? Some of the money was its own, and it borrowed some of it. Some of the money also came from the thousands of people who own a portion of the Walt Disney Company. Disney is a **publicly traded company,** which means that people throughout the world can buy and sell **stock** in it. Anyone may own part of the Walt Disney Company by purchasing shares of its stock.

Fantasia

Disney produced and released its first full-length cartoon movie, *Fantasia,* between 1938 and 1940. The project began as a short feature called *The Sorcerer's Apprentice.* Then a famous composer named Leopold Stokowski convinced Walt Disney to let him select famous classical music to use with the cartoons. It became a full-length feature animation. Apparently moviegoers thought Fantasia was too long. It cost more than $2 million but lost money for Disney when it was first released. Today, however, *Fantasia* is considered a classic. Film critics and young movie fans alike praise the animated film for its creativity.

In 1984, the Walt Disney Company hired Michael Eisner as its chief executive officer, the most important executive at the company. Eisner has brought great success to Disney in the years since he came on board.

Disney has sold stock in the company for a long time. In 1940, after the release of *Snow White and the Seven Dwarfs* and *Pinocchio,* the company found itself short of capital. It needed money to continue, so Walt and Roy offered 600,000 shares of stock to the public for five dollars each. Disney was able to raise $3 million for new projects. People buy stock in any public company because they hope that the value of the stock will increase. In other words, they hope to buy stock at one price and then sell it at a higher price later. As a successful business, the Walt Disney Company has made profits for its **stockholders** for many years.

stockholders

Individuals who own stock, or shares of ownership, in a company.

The Walt Disney Company recognized that products featuring its popular characters sold well. Today the company runs stores where customers can buy such things as costumes from The Little Mermaid *and other Disney films, the famous Mouseketeer ears, and hundreds of other fun products.*

Disney's Fearless Leader

Michael D. Eisner and Walter Disney started life in different ways. While Walt came from a humble background, the Eisners were wealthy. Michael's father was a successful attorney. Michael grew up in a big apartment on Park Avenue, an expensive part of New York City. Although the Eisners had many advantages, Michael wasn't spoiled. His parents had a rule that for every hour of television Michael watched, he would read for at least two hours.

Michael was a bright young man. His parents expected a lot from him. When he started college, he hoped to become a doctor. Before long, Michael gave up this idea. He realized—just like Walt Disney—that the entertainment world attracted him. Michael loved books, and he loved the theater. He had something else in common with Walt: Michael was not an immediate success. He held some uninteresting positions in television during college, and then for two more years after he graduated in 1964. Michael didn't give up. He sent out hundreds of letters looking for creative work. No one was interested until one of the leaders at ABC television, Barry Diller, encouraged his team to hire Eisner and put him to work making television specials.

Because he did such a good job, ABC soon promoted Eisner to more important duties. By 1975, he was one of ABC's senior vice presidents. He took ABC from last place among the three big television networks straight to the top.

In 1995, Michael Eisner (second from left) and his wife Jane (left) joined the mayor of New York City and his family at the premier of the film Pocahontas.

Then Barry Diller called Eisner again. By this time, Diller had become the chairman of the board at Paramount Pictures. In 1976, he asked Eisner to work for him once more, this time as the chief executive officer at Paramount. The company had been struggling in last place among major American film companies. Eisner committed his energies to making Paramount a winner. With Eisner at the helm, Paramount was on top in just two years.

When the Walt Disney Company offered him the position of chief executive officer in 1984, Eisner took the challenge. He brought his dedication and energy to Disney, and the result has been tremendous success.

Disney in the World

The Walt Disney® Company has its critics as well as its supporters when it comes to **corporate citizenship.** Disney®, like most large companies in the United States, wants to make sure that its customers see the company as a good citizen that helps members of its community. Some people who run large companies genuinely believe corporations, like people, should have and follow a good conscience. A good corporate citizen treats its employees fairly and protects the environment. It usually gives money back to the community or encourages its employees to do volunteer work.

The Walt Disney Company has a policy of good citizenship. Disney treats its employees well and has strong **minority hiring practices.** African Americans and women hold important positions at Disney companies. Disney hires minority writers and directors for its film and television projects.

Since 1983, Disney has sponsored a program called VoluntEARS (named for Mickey Mouse's famous ears). Every week of the year, Disneyland® employees voluntarily provide meals to the elderly in southern California communities. They help raise money for cancer research. They actively take part in community programs and work with children and young people at risk.

During 1997, in places across the United States, more than 40,000 Disney employees contributed 260,000 volunteer hours. Employees of Disney promised to volunteer one million hours by the year 2000. Some VoluntEARS work with the Boys & Girls Club of America to remodel clubhouses, take kids on field trips, and help kids with homework and after-school activities. Volunteers from Disneyland work on projects to turn vacant city lots into playgrounds and raise money for a children's hospital near Los Angeles. Three times a week, volunteers from Disney World® in Florida cook and serve meals to people who are homeless.

corporate citizenship

The belief that a corporation should be an honest member of society. A good corporate citizen treats its employees well, protects the environment, donates some of its earnings back to the community, and volunteers help in the places where it does business.

minority hiring practices

Guidelines used by a company to make sure that minorities, such as African Americans or women, have an equal chance to find work.

A young Russian child watches Disney cartoons on television. Walt Disney's characters continue to be popular all over the world.

ABC® employees volunteer their time to Habitat for Humanity, an organization that builds homes for people who cannot afford to buy one. They host holiday parties for children in shelters, work with AIDS patients, and give their time to education programs. For many years, ABC employees have worked at the Urban Women's Retreat, a safe house that helps abused women and their children escape from domestic violence.

Support for Disney's volunteer work is universal, but some people believe the Walt Disney Company does not always make the right choices. Many organizations

In 1996, MTV® held its awards at the Walt Disney Studios in Burbank, California.

*Protesters dressed as Civil War soldiers demonstrate against Disney's proposed
historical theme park. Many people worried that the park would not depict history
in a truthful manner.*

are unhappy with Disney because of violence featured
on its children's television shows. They believe Disney
should eliminate violence from all its television and
movie projects.

Other critics say that Disney's films are not always
accurate. Historians complained that *Pocahontas,* for
example, was not true to the real-life story of its heroine.
Not everyone wants a Disney park near their home, either.
Citizens of Virginia protested when the company planned
to build a historical theme park, called Disney's America, in

a rural area 30 miles from Washington, D.C. The company estimated that an additional 77,000 cars per day would travel through the area. People worried that Disney's plans would increase traffic, pollution, and noise in the area. Others worried that Disney would not take care to make the park historically accurate. The Walt Disney Company finally canceled its plans.

Other people have accused Disney of **exploiting** workers in other countries. Disney hires companies to make Disney clothing in Haiti, which it then sells at a profit in places throughout the world. Many Haitian factories pay

A group of people protest outside The Disney Store in New York City, claiming that the Walt Disney Company pays its workers in Haiti only 28 cents an hour.

The popularity of Disney characters has helped to make the Walt Disney Company one of the world's most successful businesses.

such low wages that their employees live in poverty—even when they work long hours. Critics believe Disney should either stop making clothes in Haiti, or, better yet, insist that the factories it uses pay employees a fair wage.

Everyone agrees that the Walt Disney Company has come a long way since Mickey Mouse® first appeared in movie theaters back in 1928. Walt Disney wanted his original love for animation and entertainment to live on. Toward the end of his life, Walt said, "I only hope that we don't lose sight of one thing—it was all started by a mouse!"

The question is whether today's Walt Disney Company can keep alive the imagination and vision of Walt, his brother Roy, and the others who worked so hard to build the company. With animated successes such as *The Lion King, Beauty and the Beast,* and many other highly praised films, the Walt Disney Company has reason to believe that Walt and the other founders would be proud of its success.

Important Moments

1893
Roy Disney, Walt Disney's brother, is born on June 24.

1901
Walter Elias Disney is born on December 5.

1923
Walt Disney leaves for Hollywood. He and his brother Roy sign a contract with a New York cartoon company to make animated films.

1926
Roy and Walt rename their company Walt Disney Studio.

1928
Mickey Mouse makes his debut in Steamboat Willie, *the world's first synchronized sound cartoon. Fans begin to join Mickey Mouse Clubs around the United States.*

1931
The Mickey Mouse Clubs have a total of one million members.

1932
Walt Disney wins his first Academy Award for an animated film called Flowers and Trees.

1937
Disney releases Snow White and the Seven Dwarfs.

1940
Walt and Roy decide to sell stock in the Walt Disney company to pay their debts.

1955
Disneyland opens in July.

The Mickey Mouse Club *debuts on television in October.*

1961
One of television's first color programs, Walt Disney's The Wonderful World of Color, *debuts.*

1966
Walt Disney dies on December 15. Walt's brother Roy takes over the company.

1971
Disney World opens. Roy Disney dies on December 20. Donn Tatum takes over as the chairman of the board of Disney, and Carl Walker becomes its president.

1983
The Walt Disney Company founds Touchstone Pictures, its first company that is not fully dedicated to family productions.

1984
Michael Eisner takes over as Disney's chief executive officer.

1995
The Walt Disney Company acquires Capitol Records/ABC and becomes the largest entertainment company in the world.

1998
Animal Kingdom opens in Florida.

Glossary

accurate   Truthful or free from error.

acquisitions   When one company, usually a bigger company, buys (acquires) another.

animated films   Drawings produced on film and then shown through a projector. Animated films are also called cartoons.

bankruptcy   When a company (or individual) cannot pay its debts, it may be forced to go out of business. It then pays creditors with any money is left. This process is called bankruptcy.

celluloid   A clear, plastic film that resists high temperatures. See-through drawings are placed on celluloid, and the projector light shines through it to display the images on a movie screen.

chief executive officer (CEO)   The person responsible for managing a company and making decisions that help the company make a profit.

corporate citizenship   The belief that a corporation should be an honest member of society. A good corporate citizen treats its employees well, protects the environment, donates some of its earnings back to the community, and volunteers help in the places where it does business.

exploiting   Taking advantage of someone or something for one's own gain.

media	All the different ways of communicating information to the public, including newspapers, television, radio, books, magazines, and movies.
merger	A merger takes place when two companies agree to join forces and become one company.
minority hiring practices	Guidelines used by a company to make sure that minorities, such as African Americans or women, have an equal chance to find work.
network	A television or cable company that produces programs to be shown on local stations across a large territory. The ABC network, for example, broadcasts its programs on stations all over the United States.
publicly traded company	A company that sells shares of stock to the public in order to earn money for its business.
royalties	Money paid to a company (or person) in exchange for using its property.
stock	Shared ownership in a company by many people who buy shares, or portions, of stock, hoping that the company will make a profit.
stockholders	Individuals who own stock, or shares of ownership, in a company.

Index

Items in bold print indicate illustration.

Further Information

BOOKS:

Hahn, Don. *Disney's Animation Magic: A Behind the Scenes Look at How an Animated Film Is Made.* New York: Hyperion Press, 1996.

Green, Katherine and Richard Greene. *The Man Behind the Magic: The Story of Walt Disney.* New York: Viking, 1998.

WEB SITES:

Visit the official Web site of the Walt Disney Company:
http://www.disney.com

For links to other Disney-related Web sites:
http://www.members.aol.com/RedheadFox/disney/html